MORE POWER TO YOU
A DYNAMIC GUIDE
TO SELF-MANAGEMENT

By

JANE SMITH

Editor and Consultant
Marlene Flynn

◆ ◆ ◆

MORE POWER TO YOU
By Jane Smith

Third Printing

Copyright© 1989 by Jane Smith

Published by Career Dynamics
4113 Seventh Street S.W.
Calgary, Alberta
Canada T2S 2N7

Canadian Cataloguing in Publication Data
Smith, Jane, 1934-

More power to you

Includes bibliographical references.
ISBN 1-895292-16-6

1. Self-management (Psychology). 2. Self-respect.
3. Success.   I. Title.
BF637.S8S64 1992   158'.1   C92-098155-0

Editor and Consultant: Marlene Flynn
                                Education Connectors
                                Calgary, Alberta

Coordinator: Mary Leeds
                                InterFacts Consulting Ltd.
                                Calgary, Alberta

Desktop Publishing: Sue Hauke Design
                                Calgary, Alberta

Printed and Produced in Canada by:
Centax Books, a Division of PrintWest Communications
Publishing Director: Margo Embury
1150 Eighth Avenue, Regina, Saskatchewan, Canada 5R4 1C9
(306) 525-2304 FAX (306) 757-2439

TABLE OF CONTENTS

FOREWORD

MORE POWER TO YOU provides information to make good decisions and to take positive actions in our personal and working lives. This kind of power is achieved by unleashing the resources which already exist within ourselves.

This book supplies many answers, but more importantly, it is full of questions to assist in tapping these inner resources.

Many people and many community projects have benefited from the analysis and principles Jane Smith brings to important issues and challenges. There is no more important project than ourself. Here is the guide. Enjoy.

Dr. Norman E. Burgess
Dean, Royal Conservatory of Music
Toronto, Ontario

I have been leading personal growth groups for women for twenty years. **MORE POWER TO YOU** has provided a fresh and powerful perspective to help women focus on their strengths and assets and move beyond the behaviours which keep them mired in their past.

It gives a solid base to help women assess where they currently are in the growth process, then establish both short-term and long-term goals that help them set an appropriate course. With the strategies and techniques which Jane Smith has provided, women can take charge of the direction of their lives.

E. Clair Hawes, Ph.D., R. Psych.
West Vancouver, British Columbia

AUTHOR'S NOTE

My first act of empowerment occurred when I was four years old. In my wisdom I had decided that curly hair would change my life; and so I prevailed upon the local hairdresser in Shelburne, Nova Scotia, to give me a permanent and charge it to my mother. When I arrived home my mother was enchanted with neither my hair nor my attitude, and a battle royal ensued. Whereupon I announced that due to lack of understanding, I would be forced to leave home. My mother agreed immediately, and offered me $2 to clinch the deal.

I packed a small red suede satchel and sat on the neighbour's doorstep for a while. Dr. Beveridge, our minister, walked by and ever-friendly, asked, "How's your mother?" to which I responded, "How the hell do I know? I don't live there anymore."

With great diplomatic skill, Dr. Beveridge reunited me with my family. And while all of this experience was most liberating, it did have consequences. I paid the $4.00 for the cost of the perm, at five cents every two weeks for years and I've never liked curly hair since! Thus I accepted responsibility for my actions.

As we head towards the 21st century, it becomes increasingly clear that each of us must accept more responsibility for ourself. We can no longer expect politicians to lead, teachers to look after our children's total education, doctors to be responsible for our health, churches to dictate our moral values, or employers to handle our financial security.

If you want to be well looked after, look after yourself and
MORE POWER TO YOU!

Jane Smith
Calgary, Alberta
July, 1992

Introduction

Why This Book was Written and How to Use It

You may not welcome the news that you alone are in charge of your life. You have the ability to take power for yourself, making the necessary changes that will erase feelings of helplessness. This means that you can no longer look for a scapegoat or blame others. You accept the fact that it's all up to you. You are the one. More power to you!

The first step in acquiring power for yourself is to take responsibility for your own life and feelings. How often do you hear yourself say, "You make me angry" or "That drives me crazy"? Neither the person nor the thing dictates your feelings. You do that. It's your choice to be angry or crazy. It's your attitude which dictates your thoughts, your feelings and ultimately your own self-image.

Just as your mental health is your responsibility, so is your physical health. Think of yourself as a consumer in this important area of your life. Too often you allow others to make decisions about your health because you don't feel you have sufficient expertise. By all means solicit advice from those involved in the health care field, but treat them as partners. It's all right to say to your doctor, "Although you know more about medicine than I do, I know more about me."

You have been assailed with information and advice from experts. Some of the advice from experts is good and some bad. You are the authority on you. Be selective in what recommendations/instructions/suggestions you choose. And please apply the foregoing sage advice to the use of this book as well.

Each person will use this guide from an individual perspective. After reading the first chapter entitled "Own Your Own Life", you can then decide how many chapters you'll read, in what sequence you'll read them and how much work you'll actually do. At the end of each chapter, there is an annotated bibliography for further reading. You may, if you desire, compile your own journal which will be your personal assessment of you.

HOW TO WRITE YOUR OWN JOURNAL

1. Select an attractive, blank notebook large enough to keep a journal and to include answers to the questions at the end of each chapter in this book.

2. Following the questions, write your personal resolutions in your journal. The more complete your thoughts, the better idea you will have of what changes you are prepared to make.

3. Keep notes even if they seem incomplete. What you leave out may be as revealing as what you have written.

4. Re-read your journal from time to time.

5. Remember that having a journal is a solid reminder of what changes you've made, what works best for you and what changes you still want to make.

Bill of Empowerment

Your Rights and Your Responsibilities

1. You have the right to be heard.
   You have the responsibility to make certain that others are ready to listen.

2. You have the right to your own opinions.
   You have the responsibility to allow others to disagree with you.

3. You have the right to make mistakes.
   You have the responsibility to learn from your mistakes.

4. You have the right to choose for yourself.
   You have the responsibility to be accountable for your choices.

5. You have the right to ask for what you want.
   You have the responsibility to understand that others may refuse you.

*Empowerment
is an Attitude,
Not an Outcome.*

◆ ◆ ◆

CHAPTER ONE

OWN YOUR OWN LIFE

Anyone Powerful Enough
to Give You Everything You Need
is Powerful Enough
to Take Everything You Have

OWN YOUR OWN LIFE

A scientist was watching a cocoon very carefully. He saw the Monarch butterfly struggling and fighting to be free. The scientist thought he would be helpful and snipped the top of the cocoon. The butterfly flew briefly, his wings still partly folded and dropped dead. Each push and pull would have forced the blood into his wings, allowing the butterfly's life and beauty to come into being only after his successful exit from the cocoon. In trying to make things easier, the scientist had killed the butterfly. He had taken away the butterfly's power.

Power, which comes from the Latin "to be able" is the ability to act, control or influence. When you are empowered, you are able to take control over your own life. Many people say they want to own their own lives, but they don't mean it. They actually want someone else to look after them. It is not only a duty, but a privilege to be accountable to and for yourself, for who you become and how you live.

Empowerment is self-management. While empowerment involves being totally responsible for yourself, it is not a licence to be self-centred or selfish. Nor does it mean to take power away from others. In fact, when you are empowered, you will find that you are able to deal more smoothly and effectively with others without infringing on their autonomy.

No one can empower you. You must have the courage to take power for yourself. It is helpful, however, to have a mentor if you decide to make this fundamental change in your life. A mentor is more than a friend or a role model and may come from any level of society as long as you share the same values. A mentor is a trusted guide who will challenge you, help you understand what's happening and encourage you to work through rather than avoid any painful steps in the process of making this change.

STEPS TO SELF-MANAGEMENT

STEP 1: DON'T BELITTLE YOURSELF

Keep your confidence intact. Undermining yourself is not profitable. How often do you ask yourself, "What did I do wrong?" Instead, ask yourself, "What did I do right?" Treat yourself as you do your plants and place yourself in the best possible light.

- **Live in the Present**

  Focus on yourself now, and reflect on the positive parts of your life. Don't say to yourself, "I'll be happy when I get a promotion...", or "if we buy a new house...."

- **Value Yourself**

  Don't wait for others to validate you, or to make you happy.

- **Accept Compliments**

  Some people have as much trouble with compliments as they do with criticism. The person giving the compliment has taken a risk in voicing his opinion and requires your acknowledgement. Don't ignore or reject the compliment. If a co-worker praises your presentation at a staff meeting, don't shrug it off. Let the other person know the compliment has been received, processed and appreciated.

- **Take Credit**

  Know when you have done a good job and allow yourself to be proud. In the words of Will Rogers, "If you done it, it ain't bragging."

Spend time with people who bring out the best in you.

STEP 2: DON'T BELITTLE OTHERS

Look for the good qualities in others. Undermining people is not profitable. It will neither change their behaviour nor enhance your own self esteem. You can't sling mud without losing a little ground yourself.

- **Accept Others as They Are**

  It's easy to label others as villains, be they family, friends, co-workers, adversaries, advisors, or even total strangers. Yes, these people affect you, but don't allow them to control you or your reactions. It's your choice.

- **Rely on Your Own Opinion**

  Don't base your judgement of another on the experiences of someone else. Rely on your own experiences and trust your instincts.

- **Allow People to Occasionally Disappoint You**

  Don't waste time deploring deficiencies in others when they can't always deliver what you need.

- **Be Loyal to Those Who are Absent**

- **Attend to Little Courtesies**

Spend time with people who bring out the best in you.

Step 3: Don't Allow Others to Belittle You

Eleanor Roosevelt once wisely noted, "No one can make you feel inferior without your consent." You don't have to buy into somebody's low estimation of you. If somebody is berating you, be firm, fair and friendly as you say, "I'm sorry you feel that way." Saying you're sorry about how someone is feeling is not hypocritical; it is a way to be truthful without denying your own opinion. "I'm sorry" does not mean "I'm guilty".

- **Assess the Accuracy of the Comment**

  If the comment is inaccurate, it need not upset you. If the comment is accurate, you can decide to deal with it or ignore it.

- **Channel Negative Energy**

  Don't allow blamers to get into who's right and who's wrong. Instead, help them seek a solution. Fixing the blame doesn't fix the problem.

- **Maintain a Positive Self-Image**

  If you respect yourself, others will follow suit. People always take you at your own evaluation.

- **Be Conscious of Subtle Belittlements**

  People in authority, "experts", or those close to you may tell you what you *should* do. Even if offered with the best of intentions, it does not make the belittlement acceptable. You are the authority on you.

SELF-MANAGEMENT STRATEGIES YOU CAN DEVELOP

- Recognize perfection as an impossible goal.

- Recognize high standards as an achievable goal.

- Learn to ask for what you want. Don't expect people to read your mind.

- Encourage others to ask for what they want. Don't try to read their minds.

- Don't be limiting in your description of yourself. Labels can empower you or keep you stuck.

- Eliminate "shoulds", "oughts", and "musts" from your vocabulary.

- Use "No" as a complete sentence.

- Avoid being overly competitive. Co-operation and sharing yield better results for everyone.

- Enjoy being empowered! Encourage others to become empowered!

Do You Belittle Yourself?

Answer these questions in your journal, and complete the personal resolution.

1. Do you enjoy your own company?

2. Do you constantly seek the companionship of others?

3. When you make a mistake, can you forgive yourself easily?

4. Are you your own harshest critic?

5. Do you feel you are a respected worker?

6. Do you feel you are a respected family member?

7. Someone has just said that you're looking great. Do you easily accept this compliment?

8. Do you respond with more than, "Thank you."?

9. When complimented on a job well done, do you respond with, "It was no trouble."?

In dealing with myself, I need to:

DO YOU BELITTLE OTHERS?

Answer these questions in your journal, and complete the personal resolution.

1. Are you judgmental of others?

2. Do you feel superior when you put other people down?

3. Are you a scorekeeper of who owes whom a phone call or lunch?

4. Does scorekeeping seem to be the only fair way to conduct a relationship?

5. Are you only comfortable with people whom you judge to be the same as you?

6. Are you willing to change the course of a derogatory conversation?

7. Someone has just remarked that a co-worker is the laziest person they've ever met. If you disagree, will you defend your co-worker?

8. You've been very good to a family member in need. When you are in need, do you always expect that person to respond with all flags flying?

In dealing with others, I need to:

DO YOU ALLOW OTHERS TO BELITTLE YOU?

Answer these questions in your journal, and complete the personal resolution.

1. Are you afraid of offending others?

2. Do you allow family, friends or co-workers to dictate your agenda?

3. Do people ignore your opinions?

4. To give your opinions credibility, do you find yourself quoting your spouse or some other well-known authority?

5. Do you constantly go out of your way to please family, friends or co-workers?

6. Is it easy for you to disagree with other people?

When others are dealing with me, I need to:

THE INNER VOICE

Find your inner voice. Listen to it. Hear it say:

- I don't need to be perfect.

- I don't always need to be right.

- I don't need to please everyone.

- I don't need to be liked by everyone.

- I don't always need to get my own way.

KNOW THYSELF.
THE SEVEN SAGES, 650 - 600 B.C.

REFERENCES AND RECOMMENDED READING ON SELF-MANAGEMENT

de Bono, Edward, *Tactics: The Art And Science Of Success.* Little, Brown and Co., Boston, Mass., 1984. The author, who developed the concept of lateral thinking, now deals with what makes people successful.

Ellis, David, *Becoming A Master Student*, College Survival Inc., Rapid City, S.D., 1985. Although specifically designed for students, this workbook can help you become a natural learner for your entire life. You can see yourself more clearly and choose techniques which work for you. Learning can be fun.

Helmstetter, Shad, *What To Say When You Talk To Your Self*, Grindle Press, Scottsdale, Az., 1986. Dr. Helmstetter presents solutions and techniques for use in self-management, which are applicable to professionals, students, homemakers, athletes, and leaders in every field.

Schwartz, David, *The Magic of Getting What You Want*, William Morrow and Co., Inc., New York, N.Y., 1983. The author tells you how to plan your goals creatively, approach life positively and develop a winning philosophy.

Sher, Barbara with Gottlieb, Annie, *Wishcraft*, Ballentine Books. New York, N.Y., 1979. This is a compilation of effective strategies to get what you want. It is a step-by-step plan to pinpoint your goals and make your dreams come true.

*Be as Generous to Yourself
as You Are to Others.*

More Power to You!

♦ ♦ ♦

CHAPTER TWO

BE OPEN TO CHANGE

In an Ever-Changing World
Give Change a Chance

BE OPEN TO CHANGE

There once was a poor farmer whose only wealth consisted of one horse. One day his horse disappeared leaving him destitute and distraught. The farmer approached his mentor to ask how to handle this devastating calamity. His mentor asked but one simple question, "Is it good or is it bad?"

The farmer went home to think about this profound question. The next week the horse returned to the farm followed by a herd of wild horses. The farmer rejoiced at his new found wealth and made his way back to his mentor to share the good news. The only question asked by the mentor was, "Is it good or is it bad?"

On returning home the farmer found that his only son had broken both his legs while trying to tame one of the horses. His son was the farmer's only source of help and he was deeply distressed at this turn of events. Once again he returned to his mentor and was told to ask himself the question, "Is it good or is it bad?"

The next month, the army swept through the countryside conscripting all able bodied men. The farmer's son, having been badly injured, was exempt. Shortly thereafter, the army engaged in a bloody battle. There were no survivors.

Be open to change, there's no way of knowing in advance what will work out to be in your best interest.

TRANSITION

In our technological age, change is ever present and you will find it less threatening if you develop a variety of coping strategies. The first thing you can do is not to view change as the enemy. Believe in the law of compensation:

For Everything You Lose,
You Gain Something Else

The second constructive thing you can do is to make the best possible use of the transitional phase. A transition is the passage from one condition to another. It is the interval between and a time of uncertainty. You may see a transition as a period when you don't have enough information, enough money, enough friends or enough time. It can also be a disorganized time when you are easily frustrated. This may lead you to start blaming yourself or to look for someone else to blame. Remember, being empowered doesn't just mean taking credit when things go well; it means not blaming when things go badly. Don't blame anyone else and don't blame yourself. It is not a helpful exercise and it's the last thing you need during this period.

While you cannot always control events in your life, you can control your response to them. The transitional phase is an excellent time to be proactive rather than reactive. It's a time to keep your responses in your own hands and not splatter all over the landscape.

STEPS TO A SUCCESSFUL TRANSITION

STEP 1: ADMIT YOU ARE FACED WITH A CHANGE

This may sound like very obvious advice, but many people waste time denying that a change is occurring. This denial is used to protect the status quo and to resist doing things differently. You may stick with long standing practices, even if they have been bad for you, because you considered them to be safe. It is hard work and it may even be risky to establish new practices.

STEP 2: LEAVE THE PAST BEHIND

The important time is now. Hanging on to the past, whether the tie is emotional, social or financial, prevents growth and progress. Letting go will necessitate some grieving. Stand still and feel the pain. The sooner you allow yourself to grieve, the sooner you can move forward.

STEP 3: MOVE ON TO NEW OPPORTUNITIES

It is important to remember the past and learn from it, but dwelling on what has been could cloud your present opportunities. Know yourself. Know what you want. Be proactive. Make it happen!

If you don't change, you don't grow.
If you don't grow, your world shrinks.

CHANGE

Change is inevitable. Good or bad, nothing lasts forever. Seasons change, feelings change, fashions change, relationships change and jobs change. All facets of your environment can change. It is really important, therefore, to be able to cope with and benefit from change.

Change may occur at home, school, work or in the community. Change may be upwards, downwards or sideways. Your past experience will affect how you view change, leading you to anticipate the same behaviour and results. Anticipating can lead you to make erroneous assumptions. It is a time when speculation could well replace expectation.

Even an eagerly awaited change, such as a promotion or parenthood, may be viewed with apprehension. An unwelcome change may be viewed with downright terror. In either case, it is best to take the change in bite-sized bits. Be prepared to work through the reality of the change, examine your personal goals, check out both your anxieties and possible opportunities. If you do this gradually, change can be a time of re-evaluation and growth.

STEPS TO A SUCCESSFUL CHANGE

STEP 1: BE HONEST

Check out what you really want to do and what you hope to accomplish. Sometimes this could involve turning down a desirable change such as a promotion or transfer, if it doesn't fit with your personal goals.

STEP 2: LOOK AFTER YOURSELF

This requires time and commitment. Looking after yourself means clearing time to be alone, visiting people you like and giving yourself frequent treats—buy a new book, go to a movie or enjoy a few chocolates. Talk to others who have been through a similar experience, they may provide you with valuable information. Check with others who may be affected by the change and see how they are faring. You are better off to face any possible conflicts now. Don't hesitate to ask for help if you need it. This is no time to trip over a stiff upper lip.

STEP 3: ASSESS LOSSES AND GAINS

You will know you have completed a successful change when you are able to assess both the losses and the gains.

No *change, no gain.*

TRANSITION STRATEGIES
YOU CAN DEVELOP

- During a change, a routine is helpful. If possible, keep to your usual daily schedule.

- During a change, exercise is beneficial. Your body needs all the help it can get.

- During a change, eat wisely. Don't try to save time by consuming junk food.

- During a change, set aside time for relaxation each day.

- During a change, express your feelings to those who are involved. Don't pussy-foot around, but get your concerns out in the open.

- During a change, make sure you have all the information you need.

- Some people find it helpful to write the worst case scenario or voice out loud the terrible things they think might happen, thus diffusing the fear. As Mark Twain noted, "My life has been a series of misfortunes...most of which never happened."

- Make a list of possible opportunities and at least one definite gain in your new situation.

- Be empowered. Welcome change!

DO YOU TAKE CHARGE OF CHANGE?

Answer these questions in your journal, and complete the personal resolution.

1. Is it easy for you to make a change?

2. When did you last make a major change in your life?

3. Did you resist the change?

4. Did the change upset you?

5. Was there help available?

6. Did you ask for the help?

7. Were you aware of the transitional phase?

8. Did you use it profitably?

9. How long did it take you to fully adjust to the change?

10. What could you have done differently?

11. Are you willing to create change?

12. Do you have a favourite strategy to deal with change?

In dealing with change, I need to:

THE INNER VOICE

Find your inner voice. Listen to it. Hear it say:

- I understand change is necessary to be fully alive.

- I learn from change.

- I deal actively with change.

- I look forward to change.

- I can create change.

NOTHING ENDURES BUT CHANGE
HERACLITUS, 540-480 B.C.

REFERENCES AND RECOMMENDED READING ON CHANGE

Hopson, Barrie and Scally, Mike, *Build Your Own Rainbow*, Lifeskills Associates, Leeds, England, 1986. This workbook which helps you determine what changes you want in your life, how to make them happen and what to do if it doesn't work out.

Jaffe, Dennis, Ph. D., and Scott, Cynthia, Ph.D., *Take This Job and Love It*, Simon and Schuster, Inc., New York, N.Y., 1988. This book provides information on how to change your work without changing your job. Blue-collar worker or C.E.O., all can reconnect to their personal values and vision.

Johnson, Spencer, M.D., *One Minute For Myself*, Avon Books, New York, N.Y., 1985. The author explains the secrets of looking after yourself and changes you can make in managing your most valuable asset, you.

Sher, Barbara and Gottlieb, Annie, *Teamworks*, Warner Books Inc., New York, N.Y., 1989. A step-by-step guide to turn your dreams into reality by building a success team or people network.

Wujec, Tom, *Pumping Ions,* Doubleday Canada Ltd., Toronto, Ontario, 1988. If your mind is suffering from lack of exercise, this book provides new ways of changing your attitude and conditioning your brain, just as you do your body.

CHAPTER THREE

DEAL WITH THE DILEMMA OF DECISION-MAKING

*Good Decisions Get You
From Where You Are
to Where You Want to Be*

DEAL WITH THE DILEMMA OF DECISION-MAKING

Indecision is tiring. Energy is wasted in dithering, hand-wringing and varsity-level worrying. Worrying about someone else may mean you've developed a highly exaggerated sense of your responsibility in that person's life. Worrying in your own life may mean you're hooked on perfection. Ask yourself if you have trouble making decisions because you view anything less than perfection as a failure and view failure of even the most fleeting nature as unacceptable. Worrying neither solves problems nor makes decisions.

So many decisions are made effortlessly in the course of the day that you take no notice of the process. Get up? Breakfast? Read the paper? It is, however, the major decisions which tend to leave you a spineless blob. The important thing is to make the decision and don't be afraid to be wrong. There isn't necessarily one right answer.

Thomas Watson, founder of I.B.M. says "The way to succeed is to double your failure rate." You don't have to be perfect. Give it your best shot, but don't expect perfection from yourself or others. A pedestal is no place to tap dance.

GET CLEAR

Many areas of your life may be clouded by a lack of clarity. It is mandatory to get clear in your own mind as to what you're trying to accomplish. To get clear is to know who you are, what's important to you and who has power over you.

Getting clear about what you want in and from your life will enable you to take more power for yourself. How often do you hear yourself saying, "I'm too busy."? This is just another way of saying, "I'm not clear about what's important to me." If you are constantly over-scheduled, you need to ask yourself why. Is it fear of being alone that keeps you in perpetual motion? Who is it you're trying to please with this performance?

In making a decision or solving a problem, it is necessary to clearly define the dilemma. Often the perceived dilemma is not the real dilemma; the main problem may be hidden. To get clear you need to ask yourself really good questions. Good questions are ones that open up, rather than close off, new insights and new answers.

To get clear is to see things as they really are without distortion or deceit. It is to question yourself until you can define and fully understand the main issue in any decision or problem.

Ask good questions. Ask the right people. Search for new ways to understand.

GOOD QUESTIONS WHICH LEAD SOMEWHERE:

- What do I want to achieve?

- What are my options?

- What are my feelings?

- What factual information do I have?

- Do I need more information?

- What previous attempts have I made to decide?

- What's in it for me if I don't make a decision?

- What would I like to see happen?

BAD QUESTIONS WHICH LEAD NOWHERE:

- Why is life unfair to me?

- Whose fault is it?

- Who's going to fix it?

- What do you think I should do?

THE VERY BEST QUESTION:

- What don't I understand?

THE GET CLEAR FORMAT

Using my journal, I will define an area of indecision in my personal life about which I want to get clear. This area is:

My goal is:

My options are:

My feelings are:

I have previously tried to make this decision, but:

If I don't make a decision, the benefits are:

I still need more information because:

I still don't understand:

I can use this format to "get clear" in any area of my life.

STEPS TO DECISION-MAKING

STEP 1: PAY ATTENTION

The decision making process is difficult because it often involves change. Don't feel guilty if you need time. It's okay to slow down, but don't shut down. This slowing down process will give you an opportunity to really pay attention.

- **Pay Attention to Your Day Dreams**

  Day dreams, which have been hidden away and perhaps almost forgotten, may help you get clear about how you really want things to be.

- **Pay Attention to Your Body**

  Your body sends you signals. Don't ignore it, your gut feeling may be right. The day that you're feeling gung-ho is the day to go with the flow. The day that you want to stay in bed with a sheet over your head is no day to make a decision.

- **Pay Attention to the Entire Picture**

  If you notice you are dwelling on only certain elements of the dilemma, you may misread the real problem. By focusing on all the elements of the dilemma, you will find better solutions.

*Every time you make a decision,
you exercise personal power.*

STEP 2: CHECK OUT THE EMOTIONAL CONTENT

Every decision has an emotional content. The higher or lower the emotions run, the greater the risk of a poor decision being made.

- **Watch for High Emotion**

  It is no time to decide when your scalp prickles, your face is purple and your stomach is pretzeled.

- **Watch for Too Little Emotion**

  It is no time to decide when you hear yourself saying, "Whatever you want", meaning, "I don't care".

- **Call For Time Out**

  When you feel you are dealing with too little or too much emotion, take a break.

- **Ask Yourself, "What Don't I Understand?"**

STEP 3: USE WHOLE-BRAINED THINKING

Much has been written about right brain/left brain functions. A popular theory is that the left brain is the logical hemisphere and the right brain is the intuitive hemisphere. According to this theory, left-brained people are organized, punctual, highly verbal and analytical while right-brained people are imaginative, creative and artistic. The left brain is bound up in time, processing in a sequential or a step-by-step fashion. The right brain lives in the realm of space, processing simultaneously in whole pictures or patterns.

Some cultures emphasize the left brain with preference for languages, math, reading and writing while other cultures emphasize the right brain with preference for music, dance, story-telling, acting, arts and crafts. This is helpful in understanding another culture or even another individual. How easy is it for an accountant who hates surprises, lives by rules, analyses to death and avoids risks to understand an artist who likes surprises, embraces the unknown, thrives on confusion and is impetuous?

Controversy abounds whether male and female brains operate differently and which functions are localized into which hemispheres. Generalizations are best avoided, but alternative ways of looking at problems and making decisions are necessary. Start building your reputation as an effective decision-maker. Celebrate your whole brain!

Every time you make a decision,
you exercise personal power.

◆ **Use Your Right Brain**

Sit quietly, breath deeply, listen to music and just let your mind wander. Don't force anything and still the chattering of the mind. Choose music with a 4/4 time and a tempo of 60 beats per minute. e.g. Vivaldi's "Four Seasons"; Largo from "Winter". This will relax your body, free your mind and allow you to use your intuition. If you are lucky enough to have intuition, trust it. There is nothing airy-fairy about intuition; it is a good mental model of how people think and behave.

◆ **Use Your Left Brain**

Sit at a desk, state your problem in writing and divide the page into two columns. List as many pros and cons as you can. Analyze and come to a logical conclusion.

◆ **Use Your Whole Brain**

Use your right brain to brainstorm for ideas. Use your left brain to analyze and sort out the best ideas. This whole-brained approach will allow you to focus and be creative at the same time.

A BROAD SUMMARY OF
LEFT AND RIGHT BRAIN DIFFERENCES

THE LEFT BRAIN IS GOOD AT:

- verbalizing
- organizing in a step-by-step fashion
- analyzing
- time-keeping
- understanding facts
- mathematics
- practical tasks
- following directions

THE RIGHT BRAIN IS GOOD AT:

- using imagination
- thinking in whole patterns
- creative problem solving
- risk-taking
- intuitive reasoning
- music
- design and use of color
- improvisation

DECISION-MAKING STRATEGIES YOU CAN DEVELOP

- Thought, not action, is the first step in making a good decision.

- Good decisions are based on good information.

- Don't be afraid to ask dumb questions.

- The old admonition, "sleep on it", holds true in decision making. It does give the mind an opportunity to sort and sift information.

- Make a list of the available options.

- Discuss these options with those who will be affected by your decision.

- Don't leave decisions to chance. Good decisions are not made by default; they are the result of deliberate choices.

- Every risk cannot be eliminated, but they can be minimized. Weigh the risks against the rewards.

- Empowerment promotes the ability to decide, to act and to live with the consequences.

Do You Pay Attention When Making a Decision?

Answer these questions in your journal and complete the personal resolution.

1. Do you allow others to make decisions for you?

2. By allowing events to unfold or unravel, rather than getting involved and checking out all alternatives?

3. Do you act impulsively?

4. Do you make a quick survey and then a snap decision?

5. Are you afraid of making a wrong decision?

6. Do you feel pressured when you have to make a decision?

7. Are you always rushed and feel there is insufficient time?

8. Do you avoid making decisions that are in conflict with the advice of someone important to you?

9. In making a decision, do you listen to reason, feelings, or others?

In making decisions, I need to:

What is the Emotional Content in Your Decisions?

Answer these questions in your journal, and complete the personal resolution.

1. Do you have difficulty in telling others what you want?

2. Do you base your decisions on what makes others happy?

3. Do you base your decisions on what will cause the least conflict?

4. Do you continue to collect information in order to stall and to keep the emotional content at a low boil?

5. Are you easily upset?

6. Do you always have to be liked?

In checking out the emotional content, I need to:

ARE YOU LEFT OR RIGHT BRAIN DOMINANT?

1. Do you skip around in a book rather than read from beginning to end?

2. Do you think in an orderly, step-by-step fashion?

3. Are you precise in your answers?

4. Can you express yourself well even with interruptions?

5. Do you welcome distractions?

6. Do you prefer math to art?

7. Do certain colors affect your mood?

8. Do you prefer to get the overall concept first when problem solving?

If you answered "yes" to questions 2, 3, 4 and 6, you are most likely left-brain dominant. If you answered "yes" to questions 1, 5, 7 and 8 you are most likely right-brain dominant.

EXERCISES TO DECIDE
YOUR BRAIN DOMINANCE

1. When you answer a question, have a friend check to see if your eyes move to left or right. If your eyes move right, the answer is analytical and well thought out. If your eyes move left, it is an intuitive answer.

2. When you listen to music, which ear picks up the melody?

3. When you turn in a circle, which foot do you put forward first?

4. Let your arms hang in a relaxed manner at your sides. Which arm hangs slightly forward of the other?

5. When you hug yourself, which wrist is on top?

6. When you wave your hand in a circle, do you move clockwise?

7. Which shoe do you put on first?

8. When you clasp your hands, which thumb is on top?

If your preference is always for the right side of your body, this will indicate a left brain dominance.

PLANNING AN IDEAL TRIP: A WHOLE-BRAINED APPROACH

Using your journal, write out the answers to these questions, giving the reasons for your choices. You are using your left brain.

Where will you go?
With whom? When?
For how long?

Now relax, listen to some music and visualize the ideal vacation. You are using your right brain. Have your choices changed?

Now go for a bike ride or take a walk. The theory is that movement helps you focus, concentrate and be creative at the same time.

Think about your ideal vacation. Has it changed?

THE INNER VOICE

Find your inner voice. Listen to it. Hear it say:

- I am honest with myself and others.

- I see all sides of an issue.

- I can use my whole brain.

- I can speak for myself.

- I can live with my decisions.

**FIRST SAY TO YOURSELF
WHAT YOU WOULD BE; AND THEN
DO WHAT YOU HAVE TO DO.**

EPICTETUS, A.D. 50 - 120

REFERENCES AND RECOMMENDED READING ON DECISION-MAKING

Adams, James L., *The Care And Feeding Of Ideas*, Addison-Wesley, Don Mills, Ontario, 1986. The author shows how bad decision-making habits can be broken, explains how the brain works when problem solving and that creativity involves worthwhile risks.

Fretenburg, Rae, *Getting Your Butterflies To Fly In Formation*. Vantage Press, New York, N.Y., 1982. This book will help improve self-esteem, overcome fear and set attainable goals.

Greenwald, Dr. Harold with Rich, Elizabeth, *The Happy Person*, Stein and Day, New York, N.Y., 1984. This "Direct Decision Therapy" has seven basic steps in deciding what you want in order to be happy.

Hopson, Barrie and Scally, Mike, *Lifeskills Teaching Programmes*, Lifeskills Associates, Leeds, England, 1980. This is a workbook, designed to help you in the decision-making process.

CHAPTER 4

MASTER THE MYSTERY OF MEMORY

*Memory is
the Guardian of the Mind*

MASTER THE MYSTERY OF MEMORY

Wayne Gretzky, the hockey player, has a spectacular memory. Yes, Gretzky is a marvellous stick handler and has fantastic gross motor control. But the real secret to Gretzky's success is his visual memory. He says, "I never forget anything." When he skates down the ice, he knows exactly where the other eleven players are, he keeps this filed in his brain and never loses the imagery.

Memory is an important empowerment tool. A good memory not only impresses other people, but provides you with a great deal of self-confidence. You tend to doubt yourself when you can't trust your memory. If you hear yourself saying "I think I'm losing my mind", you may actually mean "I'm losing my memory."

Memory is a person's mental record of an event. It is not an organ or a gland. People tend to refer to memory as if it were a distinct part of the anatomy, but a doctor could never look at an x-ray and say, "That's a good looking memory."

Many of us have a better visual than auditory memory. It is important for you to identify your memory style. Is it easier for you to remember faces or names? If you find remembering names easier, your auditory memory is stronger.

Once you have identified your style, you can monitor your attention span. Some people can only concentrate for short periods while others can stay totally focused for the long haul. It is helpful to distribute learning over a reasonably spaced period for longer retention. Crammed information has a limited life-expectancy because it doesn't enter your long-term memory.

Do your long-term memory a favor and stop joking about early senility or Alzheimer's. Your subconscious, where 90% of your memories are stored, doesn't know you're joking.

Most people know that the left side of the brain controls the right side of the body and that the right side of the brain controls the left side of the body. But did you know that:

◆ exercise increases circulation which provides extra oxygen to the brain and thus helps in remembering?

◆ diet may affect memory as both choline and lecithin increase the number of synapses (connections between neurons which are necessary for memory)?

Although memory is a sophisticated and extremely complex process, you don't have to understand it to use it and improve it. Most people use a tiny percentage of their actual memory capacity. Harry Lorayne, a memory expert, says, "There is no such thing as a poor memory, only a trained memory and an untrained one." This, of course, is predicated on nothing being physiologically wrong. Memory improvement is predicated as well on motivation. If you have a strong desire to remember certain things for certain purposes, you will intensify your effort. The conductor, Toscanini, memorized musical scores because he had poor eyesight and politicians will remember names because it's flattering to people and may help win an election.

MNEMONICS

Memory involves three stages. To remember information you need to be able to **record**, **retain**, and **retrieve** it. Success in all three stages is essential for remembering. Does this encourage you? Then there is short-term memory and long-term memory which are processes rather than stages. Does this help you?

Now, welcome to the wonderful world of mnemonics (pronounced ne **mon** icks) from the Greek goddess of memory. Mnemonics are aids to improving memory and were first used by Greek orators to remember their long orations. They connected major thoughts in their speeches to rooms in their homes and then took a mental walk through each room. Does that mean the longest winded Greek had the largest house?

This mnemonic used by the Greeks was referred to as the Loci system. First you memorize a series of mental pictures depicting a familiar environment, for example a room in your own house. The second step is to place the items you wish to remember in proper sequence in specific locations in the environment. This is your filing system which can be used again and again for different purposes.

An extension of the Loci system is the Peg system. The Peg uses pre-memorized concrete nouns as hooks for items to be remembered. There are several Peg systems but the most familiar is based on the nursery rhyme "One, Two, Buckle My Shoe". Memorize the Peg words:

One is a bun	*Six is sticks*
Two is a shoe	*Seven is heaven*
Three is a tree	*Eight is a gate*
Four is a door	*Nine is a line*
Five is a hive	*Ten is a hen*

Imagine that you want to remember four items to discuss at your next luncheon or meeting. You have recently received a letter from a mutual friend, you want to share the views in this morning's editorial, you are seeking information on the purchase of a new car and you want to set a date for the next meeting. Mentally place the items on the pegs. For example, put the letter in the bun, the editorial in the shoe, the car in the tree and the appointment on the door. Be sure you have given yourself enough time to make the association between the object to be remembered and the peg. Visualizing the pegs in the same way each time will help you use this mnemonic effectively.

The most simple systems are the Link and Story. The Link system is used to remember sequential items and consists of two steps. First you visualize the item to be remembered and then you associate it with the next item to form a chain. Visualizing something bizarre makes it more vivid. The Story system uses full sentences to make connections between the items while you actually develop a narrative.

The most versatile, but also the most complicated mnemonic, is the Alphabet-Number system. It represents the numbers 0–9 by using consonants which are then combined with vowels to turn the numbers into words. These words can then be used just like the Peg and Loci systems and have the added advantage of being useful in remembering numbers.

While you may not want to deliver a 60 minute oration, or remember a list of unrelated items, you would be happy to remember your best friend's phone number or the name of someone you met yesterday. The more associations you can make with information, the easier it is to remember. Finding vivid images, hooks, pegs, patterns, connections and meanings will allow you to more readily retrieve information. Stop worrying about your memory and start working on it. If you are prepared to work, you can improve your memory. As Dr. Anthony Marini, Associate Professor at the University of Calgary, states, "Memory is an intentional behaviour."

STEPS TO MEMORY IMPROVEMENT

STEP 1: BE ACTIVE

◆ Use Rhymes

"Thirty days hath September" is how most of us remember how many days in a month. Make your own rhyme for a friend's birth date, e.g. "March 8 is Jane's date."

◆ Use Acrostics

Make the items you are trying to remember form a word. The colors of the spectrum are ROY G. BIV. The great lakes spell HOMES.

◆ Use Acronyms

By utilizing the first letter of each word, you can remember a list of items, e.g. in grocery shopping, bread, oranges and butter become BOB.

◆ Read Aloud

Written material is re-enforced if both your visual and auditory memory are used.

◆ Recap the Day's Events

At the end of each day, take a few minutes to review as many events and conversations of the last 12 to 14 hours as you can.

◆ Use Memos

A note to yourself will help you keep track of an unfinished task.

Step 2: Be Attentive

◆ Really Listen

When you are introduced to someone, concentrate, repeat the name and find a connection, e.g. Mary Robins has red hair.

◆ Place Regularly Used Items in Their Own Spots

Find a convenient place in your house, purse or pockets for illusive items such as keys and glasses. If you make a change, say out loud, "I'm putting my keys on the hall table."

◆ Visualize

If you can't remember someone's name, visualize the person's appearance, when you last met, what the person does for a living, and what you discussed. If possible, use color in your visualization. It will improve your memory by as much as 50% because it makes the image more vivid.

◆ File New Information in an Organized Manner

Two helpful devices to organize new material are sequencing (placing in a step-by-step order) and categorizing (separating by color, function or some other shared attribute).

Train, don't blame, your memory.

STEP 3: BE CONFIDENT

◆ **Know What's Important to You**

Don't clutter your mind with extraneous material.

◆ **Think of Yourself as a Rememberer**

Work at remembering and let go of the fear of forgetting.

◆ **Trust and Use All Your Senses**

Memory is involved in taste, touch, smell, sight and hearing. All these senses can trigger strong memories thought to be long forgotten.

◆ **Reviewing is a Great Confidence Builder**

A reviewer's recall is much better than that of a non-reviewer. Even if practice doesn't make perfect, it will make big improvements in your memory. New material reviewed after one hour, one day, one week and then one month will be committed to long term memory.

Train, don't blame, your memory.

MEMORY STRATEGIES YOU CAN DEVELOP

- Make associations. You won't forget which humps belong to which camel if you remember that the Bactrian has two humps like the letter B and the Dromedary has one hump like the letter D.

- Practice counting to a hundred by fives and sixes and then try it backwards. Memorize a short poem each week.

- When you are introduced to someone, make eye contact, try to exchange a few words and repeat the name.

- Avoid randomization and use categories. For example, when packing for a trip, put similar items together which are required for specific occasions.

- Put your medication or your vitamins by your toothbrush or your placemat.

- Have a spot at the door for items to go.

- Have a schedule for making appointments, paying bills and ordering supplies.

- Place reminders on a mirror to catch your attention.

- Never forget: you are a rememberer.

Do You Work With Your Memory?

Answer these questions in your journal, and complete the personal resolution.

1. Can you recall your license plate number?

2. What is your earliest childhood memory?

3. Are you able, at the end of the day, to recap articles you have read in the newspaper?

4. Do you frequently say, "I can never remember"?

5. Do you use memory aids?

6. Write down three things you have recently forgotten and which really upset you. Speculate on why you forgot.

In using my memory more effectively, I need to:

THE INNER VOICE

Find your inner voice. Listen to it. Hear it say:

- ◆ I am a good listener.

- ◆ I remember anything that is important to me.

- ◆ I visualize past events.

- ◆ I use all of my senses to help me remember.

- ◆ I have a good memory.

**WITHOUT EXERCISE,
MEMORY LOSES ITS POWER.**

CICERO, 106 - 43 B.C.

REFERENCES AND RECOMMENDED READING ON MEMORY

Buzan, Tony, *Use Your Head*, British Broadcasting Corporation, London, Eng., 1982. The author deals with the latest discoveries about the brain and helps you understand how your mind works, with tests and exercises to improve your memory.

Herold, Mort, *You Can Have A Near-Perfect Memory*, Contemporary Books, Chicago, Ill., 1982. America's leading memory consultant provides simple and useful memory techniques.

Higbee, Kenneth L. Ph.D., *Your Memory: How It Works And How To Improve It*, Prentice Hall Press, New York, N.Y., 1988. This is a practical and up-to-date guide to memory improvement and deals with both the strengths and limitations of mnemonics.

Menninger, Joan Ph.D., *Total Recall*, Rodale Press, Emmaus, Pa., 1984. A good memory translates into success, promotions and achievement. It is vital to learning. Enjoyable ways to achieve a good memory are outlined along with the reasons we forget.

Salny, Abbie, Dr., and Frumkes, Lewis, *Mensa Think-Smart Book*, Harper and Row, New York, N.Y., 1986. This is a book of games, exercises and tests.

Weinland, James D., *How To Improve Your Memory*, Harper and Row, New York, N.Y., 1985. Here, simply described, are time-tested memory devices and systems.

CHAPTER 5

SORT OUT THE CHILLS AND THRILLS OF STRESS

*Stress can be Exhausting
or Exhilarating*

Sort Out the Chills and Thrills of Stress

Stress can be defined as your body's response to change. Muscles tighten, heart rate increases, blood pressure rises, extra adrenalin races through your system and the body is put on red alert. This is an age-old response to a perceived threat.

More simply put, stress is any circumstance which disrupts your life. Stress may be catastrophic as in an earthquake, a personal crisis such as a death, or it may consist of daily hassles.

A daily hassle may be tangible, for example air-pollution, or it may be intangible as in how interested you are in your job. In any event stress needs to be individually defined. Perhaps you may think of stress as a negative force which causes mental or physical illness, but stress doesn't have to be bad for you. In fact, too little stress can lead to depression, permanent tiredness and low energy.

As Hans Selye pointed out in the 1950s, the nervous system and endocrine (hormone) system prepare the body for dealing with stress in the same manner regardless of the nature of the stress. Winning the lottery, a good game of tennis, or even romance can create good stress. It's called good stress because it can be terminated at will. If stress, however, is long-term your body has no chance to rest and negative effects result.

The Chinese symbol for crisis can be translated as both danger and opportunity. It is how you perceive stress and your attitude toward it which will dictate its impact. It's your choice!

Steps to Challenge Stress

Step 1: Recognize Stress

Physical Stress Check:

___ Muscle tension
___ High blood pressure
___ Bowel disorders
___ Ulcers or other stomach disorders
___ Headaches
___ Lack of energy
___ Change in appetite
___ Allergies
___ Weight loss or gain

Psychological Stress Check:

___ Mood changes
___ Confusion
___ Impaired concentration
___ Depression
___ Irritability
___ Loss of interest in usual activities
___ Change in the way you relate to others
___ Proneness to accidents

Let laughter be your bullet-proof vest when stress attacks.

Step 2: Reduce Stress

◆ **Exercise**

Exercise is a great way to reduce both physical and mental stress. It releases the body's natural pain killers, endorphins, which help reduce tension. Exercise also increases circulation and renews energy.

Choose a form of exercise which holds your attention. Most doctors agree that half an hour 3 or 4 times a week is sufficient. You can increase the intensity and/or the length of time to suit your needs.

◆ **Develop Hobbies**

Hobbies can help you refresh your mind, body and zest for life. You can take your mind off the stressors in your life by pursuing an activity that you really enjoy. A hobby can provide an outlet for your creative ideas while allowing you to relax and have fun.

◆ **Practise Deep-Breathing**

Deep breathing is an effective stress reducing technique. How often do you find yourself holding your breath when faced with a tough situation? Follow the old admonition to take a deep breath. Don't forget to keep breathing. Concentrate on filling your abdomen and then your chest with air, exhale slowly until your breathing is regular and steady. You will feel relaxed and in control.

Let laughter be your bullet-proof vest when stress attacks.

STEP 3: MANAGE STRESS

◆ **Make Time for Fun**

Do things you enjoy with people you like. Set aside some time each day to do something that is fun for you.

◆ **Pamper Yourself**

Get enough sleep and eat properly. Manage your time wisely by setting realistic goals. Work out anger by getting involved in some physical activity. Talk out worries with someone you trust, without asking what you should do. This will help you get your problems into perspective.

◆ **Use Stress Management Techniques**

You may want to investigate meditation, biofeedback, hypnosis, visualization, yoga and massage. These all provide a relaxing experience, and need not be mystical or spiritual.

◆ **Beware of Substitutes for Stress Management**

You may wish to moderate or eliminate the use of alcohol, caffeine, nicotine, barbiturates or tranquillizers. Any relief these chemicals provide is temporary and they may interfere with your ability to stay in charge.

◆ **Look on the Light Side**

Laughter is still the best medicine. There is not much laughter in medicine, but there's a lot of medicine in laughter.

DEVELOPMENT OF STRESS STRATEGIES

FOUR POSSIBLE OPTIONS:

I Will Cope With Things as They Are

or

I Will Change My Attitude

or

I Will Negotiate With Others for Change

or

I Will Move

Stress Strategies You Can Develop

- Enjoy life and don't apologize for doing so.

- Deep breathing is one of the most effective stress reducers and can be used anywhere to release feelings of frustration.

- Use your waiting time to practice a relaxation technique such as tensing and relaxing all the muscles in your body.

- Practise visualization, which is just using your imagination, to reduce stress and imagine a desirable outcome.

- Add more laughter to your life and learn to laugh at yourself. A good laugh increases the level of endorphins in the brain and they act as the body's own natural pain-killers.

- Choose to limit the amount of caffeine in your diet. It can cause high levels of anxiety.

- Stimulate both your mind and your body. Choose an activity which is different from your day-to-day routine.

- Label breaks so you know you have had time off.

- Stress is not the enemy when you are empowered.

HOW MUCH STRESS
DO YOU HAVE IN YOUR LIFE?

The source of your stress can be found in your personal life, your job or your environment. Answer these questions in your journal, and complete the personal resolution.

1. What are the current areas of stress in your life?

2. Which of these stresses are avoidable?

3. Are you prepared to avoid them?

4. Which of these stresses are unavoidable?

5. What stress management strategies have you attempted?

In dealing with stress, I need to:

THE INNER VOICE

Find your voice. Listen to it. Hear it say:

- I am calm.

- I can look after myself.

- I live in the present.

- I don't live in the past or the future.

- I choose to be healthy.

IF A MAN INSISTED ALWAYS ON BEING
SERIOUS, AND NEVER ALLOWED HIMSELF
A BIT OF FUN AND RELAXATION,
HE WOULD GO MAD OR BECOME
UNSTABLE WITHOUT KNOWING IT.

HERODOTUS, 485 - 425 B.C.

References and Recommended Reading on Stress

Buckalew, M.W. Jr., *Learning to Control Stress*, Richards Rosen Press, Inc., New York, N.Y., 1979. The author presents ideas to help manage stress levels.

Haney, Michelle C., Ph.D. and Boenisch, Edmond W. Jr., Ph. D., *Stressmap, Finding Your Pressure Points*, Impact Publishers, San Ramon, California, 1982. The reader can develop a personalized stress management plan based on a "stress map" which shows the total stress experienced from all areas of life. Short and long-term management techniques are explained.

Hanson, Peter G., M.D., *The Joy of Stress*, Hanson Stress Management Organization, Islington, Ontario, 1985. Practical approaches to overcoming stress and turning it into a positive force are presented in an easily understood fashion.

Matteson, Michael T. and Ivancevich, John M., *Managing Job Stress and Health, The Intelligent Person's Guide*, The Free Press, New York, N.Y., 1982. The authors explain what stress is and how you can deal with it in the work place. Advice is offered to help you stressproof your job.

Shaffer, Martin, Ph. D., *Life After Stress*, Plenum Press, New York, N.Y., 1982. Ways to co-ordinate a variety of stress alleviating activities are described.

CHAPTER SIX

THE LOOKING GLASS: A REFLECTION OF YOUR NEW ATTITUDE

Put Diets on the Shelf
Put Exercise on its Feet
Set Your Own Style

PUT DIETS ON THE SHELF

People are beginning to understand that the responsibility for prevention of illness lies with the individual. As a consequence, many have quit smoking, cut back on alcohol, changed their diets, and started on exercise programs. To change your eating and exercise habits can be the first steps toward a healthier and more productive life. Let your habits support wellness, not illness.

Don't diet, but:

- Do limit sodium
- Do limit sugar
- Do include calcium
- Do limit fat
- Do include fibre
- Do include lots of water

Foods can be classified into four main groups:

1. Dairy products
2. Fruits and vegetables
3. Breads and cereals
4. Meat, fish, poultry or alternate

Choose foods from each of the four main food groups each day to maintain a well-balanced diet.

Limiting sodium, fat and sugar in your diet and substituting foods high in fibre will prevent constipation and may help to prevent colon cancer, heart disease and obesity. High-fibre foods are virtually cholesterol and fat free.

Foods high in calcium help to reduce the risk of osteoporosis and maintain normal blood pressure.

It's absolutely essential to drink water! Not only does it cleanse the body of wastes, but it carries nutrients to all parts of the body.

DIET STRATEGIES YOU CAN DEVELOP

- Drinking water 10 to 15 minutes before meals will help you feel full.

- Second helpings are best avoided.

- It's important to eat slowly and savour your food.

- Freezing leftovers immediately will help you to avoid temptation.

- Bread and potatoes are not the villains. It's the butter that will stick to your middle.

- Beware of salads with calorie-laden dressings.

- Weighing yourself every day can be demoralizing.

- Don't avoid all the foods you love, just use moderation.

- Take charge! Change your eating habits! Never diet again!

The road to good health is paved with nutrition, not diets.

DO YOU KNOW WHEN AND WHY YOU CONSUME EMPTY CALORIES?

Using your journal, keep track of all the sugar, fat and alcohol that you consume in a week, noting the time of day, amount consumed and the social surroundings. This will help you determine why and when you want these comfort foods.

	Time	*Amount*	*Type*
Monday			
Tuesday			
Wednesday			
Thursday			
Friday			
Saturday			
Sunday			

Now that you know your vulnerable times and your bad habits, what changes are you prepared to make?

In dealing with food, I need to:

THE INNER VOICE

Find your inner voice. Listen to it. Hear it say:

- I am in control of what I eat.

- I enjoy nutritious food.

- I don't have to clean my plate.

- I order wisely when I eat out.

- I choose to be healthy.

NUTRITION AND EXERCISE ARE THE TWO PHYSICIANS OF NATURE

A SPANISH PROVERB

REFERENCES AND RECOMMENDED READING ON DIET

Bailey, Covert, *The Fit or Fat Diet*, Houghton Mifflin, Boston, Mass., 1984. This employs a unique target system to help you balance your diet for the full range of nutrients while reducing harmful fat. Included is a set of basic principles, a test for all diets, a diet planner and a lifelong guide to good eating.

de Winter, Daniele, *Eat Yourself Beautiful*, Acropolis Books Ltd., Washington D.C., 1987. Nutrition, health and beauty tips are discussed, following the philosophy that feeling glamorous has a galvanizing effect on the immune system which helps to protect the body against ill-health. Recipes, with the beauty and nutritional benefits explained, are included.

Health and Welfare Canada, *Canada's Food Guide*, Department of Health and Welfare, Minister of Supply and Services, Ottawa, Ont., 1979. Daily requirements from each of the four main food groups are presented as a pattern for eating rather than a rigid set of rules.

PUT EXERCISE ON ITS FEET

Do exercise but:

- Don't overdo it.

- Don't do too much too soon.

- Don't choose activities that bore you.

- Don't choose high-impact activities unless you have discussed it with a physician.

The purpose of exercise is to increase your body's stamina and cardio-vascular efficiency, but don't put your body at risk by overdoing it. Expectation of unrealistic gain may lead to some very real pain!

Watch out for boredom. Many good intentions have been put to rest because the activities selected were dull and uninteresting.

High-impact activities can cause body injury, while low or non-impact activities are just as effective in stimulating the respiratory and circulatory systems.

Exercise is to the body what concentration is to the mind.

EXERCISE MAY BE CLASSIFIED INTO THREE MAIN GROUPS

1. Non-impact activities such as swimming, water aerobics, bicycling, cross-country skiing,

2. Low-impact activities such as walking, aerobic dance, bounding, striding; and

3. High-impact activities such as jogging, aerobics, jumping rope, squash.

Of all the types of exercise, walking is the easiest, safest, and cheapest. If you are not up for the rigours of running, walking may be the answer for you. It gets your cardiovascular system in shape, helps you to lose weight and reduces tension. Walking provides time alone or you can join a friend or a club and make it a social occasion. Walk briskly for at least 20 to 30 minutes. Use long strides and arm movement. Don't dawdle!

In order to increase cardiovascular efficiency and to ensure that fresh oxygenated blood is carried to all areas of the body, your heart rate must reach, but not exceed a certain level. To find your approximate training zone, subtract your age from 220 and multiply by 60% if you are a beginner, multiply by 70% for an intermediate level and by 85% for an advanced and maximum level.

For example, if you are 50:

> 220 - 50 = 170
> Beginner 170 x .60 = 102 beats per minute.
> Intermediate 170 x .70 = 119 beats per minute.
> Advanced 170 x .85 = 144 beats per minute.

To take your pulse, place your first two fingers on your wrist just below the base of the thumb and count for six seconds then multiply by ten. This will give you your heartbeats per minute.

EXERCISE STRATEGIES YOU CAN DEVELOP

- Before vigorous exercise, warm up with light calisthenics or brisk walking. Don't stretch until you have warmed up.

- Wearing comfortable clothing, appropriate footwear and cotton socks will increase your comfort.

- It's wise not to eat immediately before exercising.

- Drinking lots of water when exercising will help to avoid dehydration.

- Listen to your body. If you feel very hot, tired, faint, dizzy, short of breath, in pain, or cold—STOP.

- Selecting a time to exercise that is most convenient for you will help keep you on track.

- Selecting an activity which you can do by yourself and which you enjoy will help keep you motivated.

- Stretching exercises to cool down will help to prevent injuries.

- Be empowered! Develop your own exercise program! Chart your progress!

ARE YOU GETTING SUFFICIENT EXERCISE?

Using your journal, keep a record of your exercise program, selecting a form of physical activity that you can live with on a daily basis.

Check your pulse rate before you start. My resting heart rate is:

Check your pulse rate while exercising. My increased heart rate is:

	Time	*Activity*
Monday		
Tuesday		
Wednesday		
Thursday		
Friday		
Saturday		
Sunday		

Did you reach your target heart rate?

Did you feel better?

In setting up my exercise program, I need to:

THE INNER VOICE

Find your inner voice. Listen to it. Hear it say:

- I am in control of my exercise program.

- I have a lot of energy.

- I enjoy physical activity which is good for me.

- I find exercising relaxing.

- I choose to be healthy.

LET US STRIVE FOR A SOUND MIND IN A SOUND BODY

JUVENAL, A.D. 60 - 130.

REFERENCES AND RECOMMENDED READING ON EXERCISE

American Physical Fitness Research Institute, Los Angeles, California, *Here's To Wellness*, Vanguard Press, New York, N.Y., 1984. This book is a collection of positive information, put forth by a group of world authorities, to help cope with a variety of health concerns.

Liebman, Shelly, *Do It At Your Desk, An Office Worker's Guide to Fitness and Health*, Tilden Press, Washington, D.C., 1982. Included are tips for helping you sit or stand for long periods of time without pain or stiffness, exercises you can do while at your desk or waiting for a bus and ideas for helping you feel your best at work.

Ralston, Jeanne, *Walking For The Health Of It*, American Association of Retired Persons, Scott Foresman and Company, Glenview, Ill., 1986. The author discusses the health and fitness benefits of walking and how to design your own personal walking program.

Stewart, Gordon W., M.Sc., *Every Body's Fitness Book, A Simple, Safe and Sane Approach to Personal Fitness*, 3S Publishers, Ganges, B.C., 1982. A step-by step guide for planning an exercise program for people of all levels of fitness is presented in this easy to understand manual.

SET YOUR OWN STYLE

When you're feeling good, you want to look good. Increased attention, now being focused on sun protection and overall fitness, have made skin care a big item in the cosmetic business. Now many people want to use products which have not been tested on animals, are made from all natural ingredients and are pro-environmental.

You may be surprised to learn that many men have more sensitive skin than women. The type of skin you have will be dictated by your inherited factors or "designer genes". Then where you live, climate, work and life style all need to be considered.

Having said that, it is now time for you to take charge and develop a look and routine which suits you. Whether you're into a splash and dash routine or the full nine yards, certain basic steps are necessary to ensure proper skin care.

CLEANSE, REFRESH, MOISTURIZE, PROTECT

◆ Use lukewarm water because hot water is the enemy of oil. If you use soap, choose one that is clear and non-alkaline. Be sure to rinse, rinse, rinse.

◆ Your PH balance will be restored naturally over a period of time or immediately if you use a toner.

◆ In the morning, splash face with water, pat dry and add daytime moisturizer. Men may prefer an after-shave lotion or a shaving balm to close pores and sooth irritations. For dry skin, apply night cream.

◆ Apply a good sunscreen if you are going to be outside.

◆ Choose to limit your intake of caffeine, nicotine and alcohol. They are vasoconstrictors which diminish the blood supply to the skin, causing wrinkling.

WARDROBE

How you feel and the way you dress reflect a self portrait. If you feel you are dressed unattractively, you tend to hide and blend into the background. This is a dull portrait. If you feel you are dressed attractively, you tend to be more vivacious and outgoing and have more fun. This is an interesting portrait.

Steps in developing your best self-portrait:

- Clean out your closet and keep only the clothes which fit, are comfortable and attractive. Keep like items together.

- Coordinate outfits. Get rid of stray items which match nothing in your closet.

- Pick two or three colors which you really like and which flatter you. To dress conservatively, select dark colors.

- Decide on a style which fits in with your routine and activities.

- Shop with an eye for color, fabric, line and construction. Stick with natural fabrics and buy the best you can afford. Deal only with sales clerks who have time for you.

- Ties and scarves are important accessories which can snap an outfit to attention. Use your imagination and flair to make your own statement.

Fashion is what someone else decrees.
Style is what you decide for yourself.

STYLE STRATEGIES YOU CAN DEVELOP

- Wear clothing that fits you well. Choose things that are a bit loose rather than a bit tight for a more flattering effect.

- Select vertical lines and longer jackets to hide a few pounds.

- Avoid multi-colors when assembling an outfit. Pick dark tones of one color for a more slimming appearance.

- Buy good quality shoes, keep them polished and use shoe trees. Shoes should blend with the color of your hose.

- Choose long sleeves, they can be worn more places and they look better under a suit.

- If you can only afford one coat, buy a trench coat with a zip-in lining.

- Treat yourself to expensive underwear. It will make you feel good.

- Choose perfume or after shave carefully as the memory for smells is long-lasting and can be emotionally appealing.

- Be bold in experimenting with your accessories, which should accent, not dominate, your outfit. They're the props; you're the main attraction.

DO YOUR CLOTHES SUIT YOU?

Answer these questions in your journal, and complete the personal resolution.

1. Is there a dominant color in your business wardrobe?

2. Do your accessories blend with that color?

3. Do your clothes project the image you wish to convey?

4. Is dressing a pleasure?

5. Are you intimidated by well-dressed people?

6. Are you overly influenced by sales people?

7. Do you vary your clothes to suit the activity?

8. Have you cleaned out your closet in the past year?

In dealing with my clothes, I need to:

THE INNER VOICE

Find your inner voice. Listen to it. Hear it say:

- ◆ I am responsible for my appearance.

- ◆ I have a clear picture of how I want to look.

- ◆ I have good posture.

- ◆ I choose to be well groomed.

- ◆ I have the ability to create my own style.

**A FRAIL GIFT IS BEAUTY,
WHICH MUST BE NURTURED.**
OVID, 43 B.C.- A.D. 18

REFERENCES AND RECOMMENDED READING ON STYLE

Bihova, Diane, M.D. and Schrader, Connie, *Beauty From The Inside Out*, Collier MacMillan, Don Mills, Ont., Canada, Inc., 1987. This book, written by a woman dermatologist, explains the why and what of personal appearance. It looks at beauty from a scientific point of view.

Heloise's Beauty Book, Fitzhenry and Whiteside, Ltd., Canada, 1985. A collection of helpful hints which will encourage you to realize your full potential through the art of camouflage with both makeup and wardrobe.

Loren, Sophia, *Women And Beauty*, Aurum Press Ltd., London, Eng., 1984. Sophia Loren, one of the great beauties of our time, explains what makes a woman attractive, offers her own beauty tips and shares some of her personal experiences.

Miller, Clare, *8 Minute Makeover*, Acropolis Books Ltd., Washington, D.C. 1984. Here, four different images are outlined. This is a book not just about beauty, but about style.

Clark, Dick, *Dick Clark's Easygoing Guide to Good Grooming*, Dodd, Mead and Co., New York, N.Y., 1986. It includes all the advice you'll need to dress correctly for every occasion with tips on grooming exercise and diet.

CHAPTER 7

FIND YOUR OWN JOB

A Good Job Map
is Always Being Redrafted

YOUR JOB

Are you happy in your job? The most frequent complaint amongst employees is that they do not feel valued. Corporations and organizations give lip service to the empowerment of employees, to encouraging communication from the bottom up, and to welcoming suggestions and implementing employees' ideas. In reality, management would then have to give up control over employees; and many are not prepared to do so.

In the 1990's, you'll need a new compass to chart your job map. You are your own business, and are responsible for yourself.

ATTITUDES FOR TODAY AND TOMORROW

- Be responsible for your own development. Don't wait for your employer to offer further training.

- Step back and assess your performance. Don't wait for your employer's annual evaluation.

- Expect what is reasonable, not perfect.

- Look for organizations with leadership, rather than control. (Leadership is the ability to inspire and motivate people to reach their highest level of achievement.)

- Be prepared not only to change jobs, but to change industries. Follow new career paths, and retrain for tomorrow's job market.

- Define yourself by your skills, not your industry or academic background.

- Join networking groups while you still have a job.

- Always be aware of choices. When you choose, you experience personal power.

YOUR JOB SEARCH

In order to be successful in a job search, it is important to really get to know yourself, your needs and your wants. The more awareness you have, the more possibilities there are. The more skills you have, the more options there are. This type of introspection will allow you to feel more in control, more able to manage your job search and to maintain your equilibrium. While you benefit from the support of others, you are your own best resource.

Using your journal, evaluate yourself. Get to know yourself as a job searcher:

- Examine your value system. Decide, for example, the importance of creativity, money, power, helping others, and leisure time. This will help define who you are and with whom you can work.

- Assess your skills and decide which are transferrable to other occupations.

- Formulate your long-term goals.

- Formulate your short-term goals.

- Identify your options.

- Discuss your options with others.

Information is power.

RÉSUMÉS

A résumé is a written summary of all important information on your education, experience and skills tailored to a specific job. Don't have a generic résumé which serves as your all purpose pal. The résumé and a good covering letter will be your sales pitch. Make an employer want to meet you.

In preparing your résumé, remember:

- This is no time to be modest.

- Use good quality paper. Cream or light grey make a nice change from white. A non-standard size draws attention.

- Use professional word processing and reproduction services so that your résumé reflects care and attention to detail.

- Your résumé should not exceed two pages. If it is in chronological order, start with your most recent experience.

- If you have been out of the work force, or have changed jobs or fields, it is better to use a functional format, stating your skills and experience in order of importance, rather than chronologically.

- Include your volunteer work and any awards or honors. Include your interests and hobbies and non-work related experiences (for example, travel).

- Choose references carefully. Include both sexes, and be sure you know them well, and they know you well.

- Include a letter with your résumé, addressed to the person responsible for hiring—not to the company, and never to "Dear Sir or Madam". State why you want to work for the company, and why you are well qualified for the job; and the position for which you are applying, if it has been advertised.

- Request an interview in your letter, and follow up your request with a telephone call to the person responsible for hiring.

DO YOU KNOW YOURSELF?

Here is a list of adjectives which may be helpful in preparing a résumé. For fun, copy these adjectives in your journal and circle those which best describe you.

competitive	*responsible*
loyal	*enthusiastic*
flexible	*positive*
sociable	*innovative*
good-natured	*courageous*
innovative	*self-confident*
well coordinated	*calm*
compassionate	*artistic*
ambitious	*tactful*
persuasive	*energetic*
persevering	*self-motivated*
resourceful	*organized*
thorough	*well-groomed*
practical	*observant*
dependable	*punctual*

Many people use their occupation to describe themselves. It's more interesting to think in terms of adjectives, like those above, to provide some insight into who you **are** rather than what you **do.**

Your personality is an important factor in getting and keeping a job.

PREPARATION FOR AN INTERVIEW

The interview is basically an opportunity to present yourself and your interests and qualifications; and is the most critical step in the job search. It is a two-way street, and both you and your potential employer will be looking for verbal and non-verbal communications. You need to gather as much information as possible in advance about the company and the individuals who work there. This will allow you to determine if this is where you want to devote your energies, and how your particular skills can be best utilized by the company.

- Arrive early for the interview.

- Dress as if you already work there.

- Have business cards printed at a quick-print shop, using your name, address, and a telephone number where you can be reached on a permanent basis. Employers keep these on file.

- Take a copy of your résumé and a list of your references, with their positions, addresses and telephone numbers.

- Anticipate a wide variety of questions which you may be asked at the interview, and rehearse with a friend.

- Practise being relaxed. You'll blow an interview if you are up-tight and nervous. Visualize yourself enjoying the interview and see yourself as a successful applicant.

AT THE INTERVIEW

- Smile confidently at the interviewer. Pause a few seconds at the door, walk toward the interviewer and shake hands.

- Wait to be offered a seat. If no invitation is forthcoming, select a straight-backed chair across from the interviewer.

- Lean forward slightly. Don't slouch, but don't be ramrod straight.

- Wait for the interviewer to start talking.

- Be prepared to answer behavior-descriptive questions, e.g. Do your co-workers ask you for help? Do you know how to ask for help when you are frustrated on the job? You will be expected to provide specific examples from your work experience.

- You may be asked to tell in detail about your greatest success or failure in other jobs. Don't be afraid to use experiences you may have had that were not "jobs".

- Have a list of relevant questions to ask.

- If you feel the interview is taking a negative direction, don't be afraid to take charge, in a polite manner.

- Follow up the interview with a thank you letter. This not only shows you are courteous, but gives you an additional opportunity to express your continuing interest, to highlight your specific skills, and to add any new information that seems important as a result of new knowledge you gained in the interview.

ON THE JOB

- Find a mentor. This is similar to setting up an apprenticeship for yourself. Find someone you admire, who understands the corporate culture (how things are done within the company). Observe, ask questions, and be helpful.

- Be courteous. Good manners are based on consideration of others and apply on the job as well as on the social scene.

- Be well-groomed. Spend time on your appearance and dress appropriately.

- Be open to a new corporate culture. Comparison of other jobs and other bosses is unprofitable.

- Don't take yourself too seriously. A sense of humour not only helps you survive, but breaks up the tension as well. Maybe you will have to practise seeing the funny side of a situation, but it is usually there.

- Be interested in others. Make new friends, and let one of them be yourself.

- Don't forget that the most important characteristic of a valuable employee is hard work and attention to detail.

Information is power.

JOB STRATEGIES YOU CAN DEVELOP

- Sudden bursts of enthusiasm are no substitute for a plan in the job search.

- Treat your job search as a real job and devote 30 to 40 hours a week to it.

- Assess not only your skills, but your interests. Decide what you really like to do and then where you want to do it. This may lead to a decision to start up your own business.

- The job search is an information search. Use libraries, employment agencies, career centres, job fairs, newspapers, magazines and personal referrals.

- Take the initiative. Make direct contact with people with whom you want to work. Make contact with people who are sources of information, rather than job opportunities.

- Find out all you can about the company you want to work for, and match your abilities and experience to what that company's service include. Annual reports are a good source of basic facts and may be obtained from a company secretary, who can also be a goldmine of information.

- Persevere. Expect some rejection and don't take it personally. Keep going.

- Set up files. Clip articles from business magazines to keep current on the corporate scene. Include copies of all your applications and replies.

- If necessary, update your skills while you are looking for a job. Use your job search to find out what skills are needed.

- Entry level jobs can lead to promotion. Don't scorn them just because they are lower paying, or not seen as prestigious by others.

YOUR JOB PROFILE

Answer these questions in your journal, and complete the personal resolution.

- Do you know what you really want to do?

- Are all your efforts aimed towards that goal?

- Do you work against the results you want?

- Do you have long-term goals in the job market? Do you have short-term goals in the job market?

- Do you use all of your contacts? Do you cast your net wide?

- Do you rely entirely on newspaper ads in your job search?

- Do you gather information from receptionists and secretaries? These individuals can help you to find out more about the workplace and the needs of the company or organization.

- Do you see opportunities others have missed? Are you creative in removing barriers in your present job?

- Do you see barriers to your advancement in your present job?

- Do you work in any environment where you are controlled, managed, or led?

- Do you imagine how the future will look, and how your job will fit into it?

In searching for a job, I need to:

THE INNER VOICE

Find your inner voice. Listen to it. Hear it say:

- ◆ I have lots of time.
- ◆ I know my talents.
- ◆ I work hard.
- ◆ I enjoy myself.
- ◆ I celebrate!

EACH MAN IS THE MASTER OF HIS OWN FATE
SALLUST, 86-43 B.C.

REFERENCES AND RECOMMENDED READING ON JOBS

Bolles, Richard, *The 1992 What Color Is Your Parachute?*, Ten Speed Press, Berkeley, California, 1992. This is an annual designed specifically for job hunters and career changers.

Buskirk, Richard, *Your Career: How To Plan It. Manage It. Change It.* CBI Books, Inc., Boston, Mass., 1980. Goal development, productivity, women in business, the first job, changing jobs and other subjects of interest to job hunters, are discussed.

Gerberg, Robert, *Robert Gerberg's Job Changing System*, Andrews, McMeel and Parker, Kansas City, Kansas, 1986. Business Week calls this book, "an indispensable aid to the job hunter" as it offers numerous aids to an effective campaign in finding jobs. It outlines approaches for job hunting, developing interview opportunities, salary negotiation, researching companies and developing personal marketing skills.

King, Norman, *The First Five Minutes*, Prentice Hall Press, New York, N.Y., 1987. The author, a marketing consultant, takes you through the steps necessary to project the best you in any situation.

Janz, Tom, Ph.D, Hellervik, Lowell, Ph.D., and Gilmore, David C., Ph.D., *Behavior Descriptive Interviewing*, Allyn and Bacon, Inc. Boston, Mass., 1986. A structured pattern of questions designed to probe the applicant's past behaviors in specific situations selected for their relevance to critical job events.

CHAPTER 8

PREDICT YOUR FUTURE BY CREATING IT

What You Don't Become
Can Hurt You

WORK

Work is different than a job. Work is any useful effort which you expend in the home, in the community, at leisure, or with your hobbies. Work defines your place in society. You can work, and work meaningfully; and still not "have a job". Many people apologize because the work they do is unpaid. You don't need to defend work which is meaningful to you. If your hobbies, home-making, volunteer or leisure time activities satisfy you, they are your work.

Work contributes to your sense of self-worth, builds confidence, and reduces frustration. This is an important concept to bear in mind when you are planning for your retirement. You can quit your job, but do not plan to retire. You will still need meaningful work, good friends, and good health. These are exactly the same things you have always needed.

The word "retirement" has a terrible connotation. If you say you are retired, you are considered to be history. Don't think of retirement as being "the end", but rather as an opportunity to re-tire. That is, put on new tires and head out in a new direction. To make these choices successfully, you need to plan early and be aware of your resources. Then, in later years, you will have more than your memories; you will have goals and a sense of purpose.

For young people who have spent many years getting an education, the possibility of not finding work may become a reality. Even if a job is found, there is no security. Young people will have to become more creative in the work force. Contract work (in the office or at home), part-time employment, multiple jobs, and job sharing will be trends in the coming years. Developing new skills, testing new options, and creating opportunities will be the responsibility of the individual.

Traditional ideas of corporate loyalty are fossils of a bygone era. You are responsible for managing your own opportunities. Consider that you work for yourself, and ask yourself exactly what it is you do for which people will pay.

Futurist Ruben Nelson says, "To consciously shape your future, you must be able to choose wisely and act responsibly in the present."

CAREER ATTITUDES FOR TODAY AND TOMORROW

- Look to tomorrow's market and be prepared to switch work paths.

- Build skills. If you have a staff job, seek additional responsibilities.

- Seek leadership roles at work, and through volunteer activities.

- Keep visible. Don't get buried in long-term, group projects.

- Take responsibility for your personal finances. Don't place the responsibility for your financial security on your employer.

- Build a permanent network of work-related contacts and keep it intact and growing.

- Be flexible. Keep an open mind for new possibilities.

- Be responsible for your own personal and professional development.

- Set priorities.

Your attitude shapes your future.

CREATE YOUR OWN CAREER

A career is more than a job or work. It is the process of self-development throughout your entire lifetime. In order for your life to have meaning, you must perform acts which are meaningful to you. When you know **what** you want to do with your life, and why you want to do it, the **how** will follow.

A career includes all the jobs and life experiences you have ever had. Career includes education, work (paid or unpaid), volunteering, political activism, homemaking, hobbies, sports, and other leisure-time activities. It also includes the friends you've chosen and the relationships you've developed.

Career development is a lifelong process which requires management skills such as taking charge of your health and well-being, making decisions, communicating effectively, setting realistic goals, and being able to make constructive changes in a changing world.

Career development will inevitably involve changes. These changes need not precipitate a crisis, but can be thought of as a change of direction. Career changes may be of your own volition, or they may be visited upon you. While you may not have control over events, you do have control over your response.

It's never too late to create your career, which is the pursuit of personal progress, with the ultimate goal being to find that which will provide meaning in your life. Everyone wants to feel that his or her life has made a difference. To quote John Schaar, "The future is not some place we are going to, but one we are creating. The paths are not to be found, but made, and the activity of making them changes both the maker and the destination."

To create your own future, you need to develop a basic philosophical statement of why you exist. Think about the following and decide what is most important to you:

- Helping others

- Making money

- Acquiring power

- Influencing others

- Developing relationships

- Creating change in your community or the world

- Developing a specific skill

- Finding personal peace of mind

In order to get a focus on your life's mission, complete the following in a single sentence:

"I live to . . . ."

Your attitude shapes your future.

Communication

In order to create your own future, you must be able to communicate with yourself and others. Dr. Leo Buscaglia, in a recent survey, found that 85 percent of the people who responded agreed that the attribute most highly prized was the ability to communicate. It ranked ahead of honesty, compassion and affection. At home, on the job, in the community, or socially, effective face-to-face interaction is the key to success. This is your opportunity to impart, and receive, ideas and information.

Communication is a two-way street. Many people confuse the ability to talk with the ability to communicate. If you're too busy broadcasting, you're not doing much receiving. Conversely, if you're doing all the receiving, you're not contributing. Many people operate on the assumption that, in conversation, the first person to take a breath automatically becomes the listener. Be courteous in conversation; and, if you disagree, do so without being disagreeable. The magic words of communication are, "Tell me more."

Few people enjoy being alone most of the time. Everyone wants someone to listen. If you want to be heard, in your speaking:

- Speak neither loudly nor too softly.

- Pause to give others a chance to respond.

- Have more than one topic. Do not dwell on the weather, or worse, on yourself or your children.

- Be genuine. Be honest in what you say.

- Be consistent. Match your words to your facial expression and body language.

- Be fair. Don't let prejudices and stereotypes get in your way.

In your listening, remember that listening involves more than not speaking. If you want to be a good listener:

- Heed Miller's Law: "In order to understand what another person is saying, you must assume that what they are saying is true" (George Miller, psychologist). This does not mean you **accept** what has been said as true, but you merely assume it to be true for the purpose of communication.

- Give your full attention to the speaker. Be courteous and enthusiastic.

- Don't interrupt or keep changing the subject.

- Be non-judgmental.

- If you disagree with the speaker, stay neutral, rather than becoming emotional.

Effective communication skills involve:

- **Negotiation.** This sets out the playing field and the rules for "where, when, and how".

- **Active listening.** This involves more than hearing, and requires your undivided attention.

- **Giving feedback.** This is a summary of what you have heard and is a seeking of confirmation.

- **Body language.** This is not just posture. It is all of your actions and gestures, which may speak louder than words.

- **Tone of voice.** How you say something may be more important than what you say.

- **Silence.** This need not be a period of discomfort, but allows the speaker time to proceed at his or her own pace.

- **Eye contact.** This expresses interest and a desire to listen.

- **Good questions.** This means using questions that are open-ended, and can't be answered with a "yes" or "no".

One of the most important people you need to communicate with is yourself. It is truly amazing how much information you will discover if you take time to explore your internal world. This means taking time for yourself, being alone, and being quiet. Many people talk to themselves, silently or out loud, but how many consciously listen to their thoughts. Finding the inner thought or voice takes practice. But if you don't look, you won't find it. You need to practice every day, preferably at the same time and in a quiet place. Your inner voice will know what's best for you and will expect you to conform to your image of yourself, rather than living to fulfill the expectations of others. In this form of communication:

- Be honest with yourself.

- Be curious.

- Be non-judgmental. Quit blaming yourself.

- Be attentive to your needs.

- Be detached, and step back in assessing your needs.

- Be positive. Choose your words carefully.

- Be specific. State the details.

Are You an Effective Communicator?

Work with a friend. Each of you will prepare a view on a topic about which you will disagree. For example, you might use such a statement as "Daycare should be universal", or "Marriage is no longer viable". Take turns giving your points of view. Before you respond to the other person, you must summarize what you heard the other person say. When the other person is satisfied with your accuracy, you may make your own point. After ten minutes, stop and discuss these questions.

For the speaker:

1. Was this a difficult topic for you?

2. Did you speak logically, avoiding complications?

3. Did you speak clearly and vary your tone of voice?

4. Did you establish eye contact?

5. Did you use a friendly tone of voice?

For the listener:

1. Was this a difficult topic for you?

2. How easy was it for you to listen when you had so much you wanted to share?

3. Were you attentive and respectful?

4. Did you establish eye contact?

In communicating with others, I need to:

DO YOU KNOW WHAT YOU LIKE?

In your journal, write out your ideas on the following questions:

1. Outline a typical day's routine.

2. Which tasks gave you the most pleasure?

3. Which tasks gave you the least pleasure?

4. Which tasks were you best equipped to perform?

5. Which tasks were you least equipped to perform?

6. Do your interests in (2) match your skills in (4)?

DO YOU KNOW WHAT'S IMPORTANT TO YOU?

1. Do you think you have the right education?

2. Do you think you live in the right place?

3. Do you think you have the right mate?

4. Do you think you are a success?

5. Name three important things you have accomplished which you feel are indicators of your success.

6. At this point in your life, what do you want to accomplish?

7. At this point in your life, what is it you want to acquire?

8. If you knew you were going to be struck by lightning in a year, would your list of projected accomplishments and acquisitions change?

9. If you knew you were going to inherit a million dollars in a year, would your list of projected accomplishments and acquisitions change?

When creating my career and dealing with what is important to me, I need to:

THE INNER VOICE

Find your inner voice. Listen to it. Hear it say.

- ◆ I have a personal philosophy.

- ◆ I am resourceful.

- ◆ I am autonomous.

- ◆ I am congruent.

- ◆ I create my future.

**NO MAN IS HAPPY
UNLESS HE BELIEVES HE IS.**
PUBLILUS SYRUS, 50 B.C.

REFERENCES AND RECOMMENDED READING ON CREATING YOUR FUTURE

Bolles, Richard, *The Three Boxes of Life and How to Get Out of Them*, Ten Speed Press, Berkeley, California. This book calls for a change in the way we think about school, work, and retirement. Learning, working, and playing are lifelong and simultaneous activities rather than boxes and call for a restructuring of our work lives.

Peck, Scott M., M.D., *The Road Less Travelled*, Simon & Schuster, New York, New York, 1978. Dr. Peck suggests ways in which problems can be confronted and resolved in order to change and reach self-understanding.

Toffler, Alvin, *Powership*, Bantam Books, Toronto, Ontario, 1990. While there have been shifts of power at the global level, equally significant shifts are taking place in the everyday world we inhabit. The author has formulated a comprehensive synthesis about the fast-arriving civilization of the twenty-first century. A powershift does not merely transfer power. It transforms it.

Thompson, Charles, *What a Great Idea!*, Harper Collins Publishers, New York, New York, 1992. You'll learn proven, flexible techniques that can help you generate ideas immediately and you will become empowered to make creativity a more conscious and powerful part of your life and work in the coming century.

Think of Your Life
as Your Career
and Make it a Work of Art.

More Power to You!

♦ ♦ ♦

CHAPTER 9

SUMMARY

SUMMARY

DEVELOP SELF TRUST

Helplessness is learned. Empowerment is also learned. If you believe you have power, or if you believe you don't have power, you will always be right. The empowered person is self-sufficient, self-reliant, accepts responsibility for his or her life, and is not easily manipulated by others, even by experts or authority figures.

Self-trust may well be the most important self-management tool you'll ever discover. Once you have faith in yourself, you are prepared to take small steps into the unknown.

Take change in bite-sized bits. If you have trouble asking for help, the next time you are on an elevator, ask someone to push the button for you. If you have trouble saying "no", on the next request say, "I can't do that right now." If you always buy the cheapest brand for yourself, on your next shopping trip buy the most expensive box of Kleenex. If you always splurge, try a few sale items. If you have trouble making conversation in social groups, try talking to someone in a queue.

One small change can have a ripple effect. If your change one ingredient in a scientific experiment, other changes will occur as a result. If you change one belief about yourself, you can begin to change your life.

BEWARE OF PERFECTION

Leave perfection to the Olympic Games. The closest you'll come to perfection is when you fill in a job application. Strive for improvement. Perfection brings with it a lot of baggage in the form of the three Ps: panic, procrastination, and paralysis. It comes in four guises: appearance, performance, relationship, and moral.

Is anything less than perfection considered a failure? Is it better to do nothing? Delay and postponement are barriers to accomplishment. And where is joy, if you feel your own personal best isn't good enough? Once you face your own imperfection, you will be more tolerant of the failings of others.

BE AWARE OF OTHERS

Empowerment is not a licence to be self-centred or selfish. It is not blowing out another's candles so that yours will shine more brightly. It is not only awareness of self, it is awareness of others. It means caring about others, but not accepting responsibility for their problems. To do so is to diminish the other person; the message may be "I'm smarter than you". It's better to offer information than advice thereby allowing others to solve their own problems.

I'm Not Perfectly O.K.,
You're Not Perfectly O.K.,
but that's Perfectly O.K.

◆ ◆ ◆

STRATEGIES FOR OWNING YOUR OWN LIFE

1. Remind yourself about what you've achieved. Talk constructively to yourself, using a positive inner voice.

2. Learn to look after yourself. Keep fit, and find relaxation techniques that work for you.

3. Gather, share, and analyze as much information as you can, on any topic in which you're interested or about which you have to make a decision. Look at the whole picture.

4. View change as a beginning, rather than an ending.

5. Get clear about who you are, and come to grips with your basic value system. Be specific.

6. State your own vision of what you want your life to be. Let your vision be imaginative and inspired. Let it state the ideal.

7. State your goals which are more earth-bound and realistic than your vision. Be willing to re-evaluate these goals, but leave your vision intact.

8. Be responsible for your own life, and encourage others to do the same.

9. Monitor your progress. If you've kept a journal, review and repeat the exercises. This will provide "quality control" for you.

10. Use experts (lawyers, doctors, accountants) as consultants, and not as the ultimate authorities. If their advice is not in agreement with your basic value system and what you feel to be right, walk away. You must "go with your gut".

11. Be courteous. Courtesy is more than etiquette. It's an active respect and caring for others.

12. Learn to take yourself less seriously. Humour is a metaphor for all positive emotions and is a wonderful filter through which to view the world.

13. Beware of the perfection trap.

14. Always be aware of choices. Anytime you make a choice, you have exercised personal power.

These are just some of the tools and strategies
through which you can own your own life.
Others you find for yourself
may be even more valuable.

MORE POWER TO YOU!

If You Want to Be
Well Looked After,
Look After Yourself.

More Power to You!

◆ ◆ ◆

Share *MORE POWER TO YOU* with a friend

MORE POWER TO YOU is $15.95 per book, plus $2.50 (total order) for shipping and handling:

Number of books _____ x $15.95 = $ _____

Postage and handling _____ = $ _2.50_

Subtotal _____ = $ _____

In Canada add 7% GST _____ (Subtotal x .07) = $ _____

Total enclosed_____ = $ _____

U.S. and international orders payable in U.S. funds./ Price is subject to change.

NAME: _____

STREET: _____

CITY: _____ PROV./STATE _____

COUNTRY _____ POSTAL CODE/ZIP _____

Please make cheque or money order payable to: **Career Dynamics**
4113 Seventh Street S.W.
Calgary, Alberta
Canada   T2S 2N7

For fund raising or volume purchases, contact **Career Dynamics** for volume rates.
Please allow 2-3 weeks for delivery

Share *MORE POWER TO YOU* with a friend

MORE POWER TO YOU is $15.95 per book, plus $2.50 (total order) for shipping and handling:

Number of books _____ x $15.95 = $ _____

Postage and handling _____ = $ _2.50_

Subtotal _____ = $ _____

In Canada add 7% GST _____ (Subtotal x .07) = $ _____

Total enclosed_____ = $ _____

U.S. and international orders payable in U.S. funds./ Price is subject to change.

NAME: _____

STREET: _____

CITY: _____ PROV./STATE _____

COUNTRY _____ POSTAL CODE/ZIP _____

Please make cheque or money order payable to: **Career Dynamics**
4113 Seventh Street S.W.
Calgary, Alberta
Canada   T2S 2N7

For fund raising or volume purchases, contact **Career Dynamics** for volume rates.
Please allow 2-3 weeks for delivery

Share *MORE POWER TO YOU* with a friend

MORE POWER TO YOU is $15.95 per book, plus $2.50 (total order) for shipping and handling:

Number of books _____x $15.95 = $ _____

Postage and handling _____ = $ _2.50_

Subtotal _____ = $ _____

In Canada add 7% GST _____(Subtotal x .07) = $ _____

Total enclosed_____ = $ _____

U.S. and international orders payable in U.S. funds./ Price is subject to change.

NAME: _____

STREET: _____

CITY: _____ PROV./STATE _____

COUNTRY _____ POSTAL CODE/ZIP _____

Please make cheque or money order payable to: **Career Dynamics**
4113 Seventh Street S.W.
Calgary, Alberta
Canada   T2S 2N7

For fund raising or volume purchases, contact **Career Dynamics** for volume rates.
Please allow 2-3 weeks for delivery

Share *MORE POWER TO YOU* with a friend

MORE POWER TO YOU is $15.95 per book, plus $2.50 (total order) for shipping and handling:

Number of books _____x $15.95 = $ _____

Postage and handling _____ = $ _2.50_

Subtotal _____ = $ _____

In Canada add 7% GST _____(Subtotal x .07) = $ _____

Total enclosed_____ = $ _____

U.S. and international orders payable in U.S. funds./ Price is subject to change.

NAME: _____

STREET: _____

CITY: _____ PROV./STATE _____

COUNTRY _____ POSTAL CODE/ZIP _____

Please make cheque or money order payable to: **Career Dynamics**
4113 Seventh Street S.W.
Calgary, Alberta
Canada   T2S 2N7

For fund raising or volume purchases, contact **Career Dynamics** for volume rates.
Please allow 2-3 weeks for delivery